"This book is dedicated to all teenagers across the globe. No matter your age, your gender, your race...No matter where you live or what language you speak. You're not alone. We will all have different destinations. But we are all connected through the same journey. Your struggle is your story, and your story is your strength. The world is yours."

—*Daniela Lozano*

Copyright © 2019 24/7 Teach—All Rights Reserved—This book or any portion thereof, may not be reproduced or used in any manner whatsoever without the express permission of the publisher and author, except for the use of brief quotations in a book review.

Table of Contents

Chapter 1: **What Are Social Skills?**..p.1-2

Chapter 2: **Peer Pressure**...p.3-5

Chapter 3: **Stage Fright**..p.6-8

Chapter 4: **Heartbreak**...p.9-11

Chapter 5: **Academic Breakdown**...p.12-15

Chapter 6: **Catfishing**...p.15-19

Chapter 7: **Bullying**...p.19-22

Chapter 8: **Body Image**..p.23-27

Chapter 9: **Isolation**..p.28-31

Chapter 10: **Over to You**..p.33-32

What Are Social Skills?

"I remember being a teenager and feeling misunderstood. I would look in the mirror and feel self-conscious. I would struggle on a math test and feel ashamed. I would ride the school bus and feel afraid. I remember losing friends and feeling betrayed. By the time I turned 13, suddenly the world seemed to be working against me. I quickly came to learn the word "teenager" was a negative reference in our society instead of the identification of a human being. I was inevitably stereotyped as "rebellious," "spoiled," or "clueless." Society has always been quick to opinionate *why* teens need to change and *who* they ought to be. However, despite society's pointed fingers and condescending looks, teenagers are never actually taught how to appropriately solve the challenges they face. Perhaps, it's because their adult counterparts were never taught how to do it either. As a teen, I remember assuming there would never be a light at the end of the tunnel. But there was. Today, as an adult, I can look back now and say with certainty that society was never the answer to my teen problems. The real answer existed in the form of *social skills*."

Social skills are the learned abilities and behaviors needed to successfully work through the challenges of everyday life. These skills are not just for "survival" or mere "common sense." These are the critical life skills you will need to thrive and flourish as an individual. Whereas *technical skills* are concrete, *social skills* are abstract and serve as the implied, invisible rules of society. Although social skills include things like being respectful, honest, kind, and patient—they also encompass more than just good manners. Efficient **communication**, **problem-solving**, **organization**, and **interpersonal** skills are all core components of the social skill set as a whole. Mastering social skills can further help you develop other important life skills, such as those needed to perform basic, day-to-day management. For example, good social skills can help you manage money, cook, date, maintain a home, repair a car, or raise a family. As a child, social skills can help you form friendships. As a teen, they can help you resolve conflict. As an adult, social skills can help you land your dream job.

Throughout your lifetime, social skills will help you with all three scenarios combined—as well as with much more. Social skills are taught, learned, and practiced much in the same way as are academic skills. Both sets of skills can be acquired through a repeated process of **seeing**, **thinking**, and **doing**. However, unlike with academic skills—social skills are not as thoroughly emphasized within our school curriculum. This lack of education is both ironic and counterproductive

given that the majority of our lives' socialization occurs in the school setting. There exists a wrong and widely circulating assumption that these skills are "soft" and "easy"—and therefore, do not need to be reinforced within the traditional education system. Society assumes efficient social skills' training is a phenomenon that can occur on its own. It is assumed we will naturally acquire social skills from the minute we are old enough to walk, talk, and interact with surrounding stimuli and environments. As a result of these assumptions, our education system neglects social skills' training in favor of more profitable time investments, such as training for standardized testing.

This shifts the responsibility of social skills' training to parents or even to the children themselves—who are often forced to figure it out on their own. Yet, the truth of the matter is that social skills are subtler than academic skills, and therefore require a more supportive, holistic, and direct approach to teach them. *Social intelligence*—also known as *emotional intelligence*—is equally as important to our life success as is academic intelligence. In many cases, it's an intelligence that is just as hard (if not harder) to acquire as the one taught in our schools. It's no coincidence the majority of teens identify school as a primary cause of anxiety, fear, and uncertainty. In fact, it is fairly common for adults to struggle in social situations, as well. In both circumstances, the dilemma can be traced back to a person's absence of social skills' training within their childhood or adolescence. Underdeveloped social skills can leave us vulnerable to low self-esteem, no matter our age. Poor social skills inhibit our ability to solve real-world problems and our ability to cope with life outside the confines of a classroom.

When we fail to develop social skills, we limit ourselves to having average, even dreadful life experiences instead of having the best. Strong social skills can help us become resilient and independent people in school, home, work, and everywhere else. Most importantly, effective social skills can help us win at life. As a teen, you're going through countless changes that can make your life feel like a constant war zone. Everything around you is changing and it's not unusual for you to feel a little lost or uncertain of your capability to keep up. You will approach new, exciting, and sometimes intimidating scenarios that will result in plenty of cringeworthy moments. Each teen's reaction to these unfamiliar scenarios will be unique and maybe even a little awkward. That's normal. But being a teenager is also a once-in-a-life-time experience. It'll soon be over, and you'll wish you had enjoyed it more instead of focusing on trivial insecurities. If *confidence* is the key to conquering teen life, then *social skills* are the key to becoming *self-confident*. If you're dealing with low self-esteem, fear no more. Here's your ultimate guide to surviving those awkward teen moments.

Awkward Moment #1: Peer Pressure

Peer pressure is the "feeling that one must do the same things as other people of one's age and social group in order to be liked or respected by them."[1] Your peers can directly influence you to change your behaviors, attitudes, and values to conform to those of the rest. This influence can either be positive or negative depending on the action you are being pressured to do. For example, when your peers encourage you to study for better grades or to practice for a better athletic performance—you are being positively influenced. However, when your peers persuade you to do things like skip class or lie to your parents—you are being negatively influenced. Peer pressure may take place through various forms. Sometimes it is verbally expressed or communicated via body language. Other times, it takes place in the form of subtle, ***social cues*** or signals—such as through your peers' approving or disapproving facial expressions.

Moreover, some negative peer pressure effects will be more harmful than others. For instance, being pressured to cheat on a test will result in more serious consequences than being pressured to dress or to talk a certain way. Throughout your adolescence, you will be spending more time at school with your peers, than at home with your family. Your decisions will be naturally affected by how you identify with these peers. You will be watching what others are doing, desiring what others have, and admiring the peers you perceive as "popular." But the desire to fit in and gain acceptance can place you in risky situations and get you into a lot of trouble. You might experience peer pressure from a stranger, your crush, and sometimes even from your best friends. The worst part about is that you are probably doing something illegal. Many teens are influenced to try drugs, alcohol, or tobacco. Some are pressured to get tattoos or piercings. Others are pressured to shoplift or to exchange inappropriate photos via text.

Negative peer pressure is all about doing something you don't want to do. Teens who are insecure are more likely to give into negative peer pressure, as opposed to those with high self-confidence. Yielding to negative peer pressure does not make you cool or popular—it makes you a follower. But being a positive influence will make you the leader of your peer group. You can win the approval and respect of your peers without having to do anything you're uncomfortable with. When you guide and motivate others to do the right thing— you instantly become a role model. Mastering ***leadership*** will help you combat peer pressure with confidence. Leaders dare

---

[1] Definition of *peer pressure* in the Merriam-Webster dictionary.

to be different and aren't afraid to stand apart from the crowd. Become someone your peers can admire by having strong *principles* and *values* others cannot break. It can be hard to be the first or only person to say "no" during a peer pressure situation—but with courage, it can be accomplished.

Don't ignore your gut instincts 👍 Paying attention to your *feelings* can help you prevent negative peer pressure. If a decision you are about to take *feels* wrong, it's probably because it is. You can avoid peer pressure altogether by leaving a situation before anyone can tempt you to do something dangerous. If something doesn't feel safe—walk away. This is the best thing you can do if you encounter peer pressure alone.

Choose your friends wisely 👍 You've probably heard your parents or teachers tell you this before, and there is great reason and truth behind it. For example, if the people within your social circle do not engage in underage drinking or texting and driving, you are probably not doing these illegal activities either—even if you see other teens do them. It's important to choose friends with your same values and morals—so you can stand up against peer pressure together. Pick friends who will strengthen your *self-control*, speak up for you, and support you when you choose to resist bad influences. The right friends will never force you to explain or apologize for a *good* decision. All it takes is one other person who feels the same way as you, to weaken the power of negative peer pressure. If you always find yourself in problematic scenarios, it might be time to drop your current social group and get some new friends.

Plan for potential situations 👍 Unfortunately, you can't always avoid negative peer pressure. As a teen, you will be exposed to many tricky situations in the same places where you go to socialize. Let's say, you want to go to a party, but think you might be pressured to try alcohol or to engage in risky sexual activity. In these cases, you will need to brainstorm ahead of time on how you will combat each and every pressure point. Plan out your decisions and create a "safety" code that only you and your friends or parents will recognize. For example, if you feel unsafe while chatting with a boy at a party, you can tell your friend, "Hey, I think I left my jacket in your car. Can we go get it?" Or, if you are being offered drugs and want to leave a party—call your parents and say, "Hey, can you give me a ride home? I have a bit of a headache." There are plenty of safety codes you can invent to evade looking "uncool" in front of your peers.

Practice tricks and phrases 👍 "Asking 101 questions," can successfully stop someone from pressuring you. Suppose someone wants you to try tobacco. You can begin asking this person questions like, "How long have you been trying tobacco? Are you addicted? Why do you do it? What do your parents think about it? Doesn't tobacco give you bad breath?" Continue asking questions until your peer becomes annoyed or exhausted and leaves you alone. Furthermore, take your own beverage (such as soda or water) to a party—to avoid accepting an alcoholic one. Your peers will be less likely to offer you a drink, if they see you already have one in your hands. You can also combat peer pressure with excuses such as, "I have a running competition coming up and I can't afford to be slow. Smoking will kill my lungs." Or, "One of childhood friends died of a drug overdose. I don't want to repeat another tragedy." Or, "I have a really jealous boyfriend. I don't think he'll like me being alone with you."

If peer pressure continues to trouble you, reach out to a trusted adult for help. Talking to your parents, a teacher, or a school counselor can help you combat peer pressure. Do not let a mistake make you feel ashamed or stop you from getting help. Resisting peer pressure is tough. But with self-confidence, you can become the *leader* of your pack.

Awkward Moment #2: Stage Fright

Stage fright—or ***performance anxiety***—is the "feeling of fear or nervousness that some people have just before they appear in front of an audience."[2] Stage fright can happen when you need to present in front of your classmates, when your teacher chooses you to answer a question, or when you have to schedule an appointment over the phone. But stage fright also occurs during nonverbal activities, like competing in a sport or simply walking into the school cafeteria. Some teens experience stage fright to a lesser degree than others. Teens who like being the center of attention will find it easier to be in front of an audience, as opposed to shy and reserved teens. Nonetheless, stage fright affects everyone from public speakers to musicians to athletes. It even affects grown-ups in the same measure as it affects teens. For instance, it's not uncommon for an adult to get stage fright during job interviews. The result is always the same. You feel all the world's eyes are on you—waiting for you to make a mistake. Sometimes stage fright becomes so unbearable that you might quit your favorite hobby or risk a bad grade in class to purposefully avoid performance scenarios.

Stage fright can significantly affect your self-confidence and lower your ability to lead a normal life. Although a small level of stage fright is normal in everyone, if your reactions are excessively intense and turn into full-blown panic attacks—it's time to overcome this problem. If left untreated, severe stage fright can lead to more serious problems such as social phobias, mental disorders, or poor physical health. Some common symptoms of stage fright include headaches, stomachaches, a racing heart, shaking hands, tightening in the chest, tense muscles, dizziness, and nausea. You might experience a cold-sweat breakout, "butterflies" in your stomach, or the need to quickly escape a room. Stage fright is your body's **"flight or fight"** response to *perceived* danger. But because there is no real threat to your safety when speaking or performing in front of an audience—this response is both unreasonable and unrealistic. Any negative thoughts or exaggerated feelings of worry can worsen your body's natural response to unfamiliar settings.

For this reason, it's important to understand and reveal your subconscious fears related to stage fright. Why does being seen and heard frighten you? For example, are you scared of being rejected? Are you scared of displaying vulnerability? Or are you scared of not being perfect? A need to prove yourself to others is usually at the very root of stage fright. It's OK to feel uncomfortable, but do not let your fear stop you from accomplishing a goal. Avoiding

---

[2] Definition of *stage fright* in the Collins English Dictionary.

challenges may give you fast relief but will actually worsen your fear in the long run. Your life will always be full of situations in which you will be forced to step outside your comfort zone. As an adult, you will be regularly expected to speak in public—whether it be to present an academic thesis or to pitch an idea to a team of executives. In fact, **effective communication** is a skill that will make you highly marketable to your future employers. Therefore, it will be wise of you to start tackling stage fright now, as a teen. Learn to view each performance challenge as an opportunity for growth, instead of doom. Fortunately, there are many ways to overcome stage fright.

Breathing techniques Practice relaxed and controlled breathing five minutes before any type of performance. Closing your eyes and counting backward to 10 can really help you get focused. Take deep, slow breaths as you inhale and exhale. During *diaphragmatic* breathing, you should relax your shoulders and breathe through your nose. If executed correctly, your chest will remain still while your abdomen expands.[3] Other strategies, such as meditation, can further help you moderate your anxiety and stress. Make it a routine to practice your preferred relaxation technique at least three times every day.

Recite a mantra Modify and transform your negative thoughts into powerful, positive phrases. Each time you hear yourself saying, "I'm going to make a fool out of myself"—tell yourself—"No. The only person I need to impress is myself. I am going to be the best that I can be." Change the fearful voice in your head to a confident one. Mantras are inner thoughts such as "I can accomplish anything I set my mind to," or "What doesn't kill you, makes you stronger." Come up with your own motivational phrase to repeat several times before any big performance.

Visualize your success Mentally rehearsing your performance beforehand can truly help you manifest your real-life success. Visualizing your performance is an expansion of the mantra strategy. Clear your head of all self-doubts and concentrate on positive outcomes. Do not think about what could go *wrong* during your performance. Instead, think about all the things that could go *right*. Close your eyes, get centered, and mentally picture each phase of your performance. Imagine your audience is smiling and cheering for you. Let's say, you will be presenting an important project in front of your entire class and are very nervous. To calm yourself, visualize how everyone in the room will eagerly stand up and clap for you by the time you speak your last word.

---

[3] Diaphragm breathing basics according to Healthline.

> **Practice makes perfect** ✏️ As scary as it might sound, stage fright can only be overcome through more practice with performance scenarios. One of the most common causes of stage fright is *public speaking*. Mastering *public speaking* will not only help you with verbal situations, but also with physical ones that require confident body language. The key to public speaking is preparation, good posture, proper voice modulation, and being yourself. Smile, make strong eye contact, and make an attempt to emotionally connect with your audience through your tone. Pretend you are speaking to your close friends instead of to a big room of spectators. Start off with baby steps by practicing with people you are comfortable with, like your family. You can even practice in front of a mirror or by recording a video of yourself speaking. A process of trial and error will help you overcome your fears and eventually perfect your performances.

It's important to know that stage fright is usually a fleeting fear that diminishes as you progress with your performance. Its worst effects occur right before you start. If you can survive this brief moment, then you will definitely be able to survive the rest. Relieve any pre-performance tension by shaking out your muscles, taking a short walk, or by jumping up and down. The next time you feel embarrassed, remember that the focus of any performance will always be on the audience—not on you.
Your audience is *rooting* for you—*not judging* you. If all else fails, you can always **"fake it 'til you make it."** Pretend to be completely sure of what you're doing—and watch yourself slowly become truly self-confident.

Awkward Moment #3: Heartbreak

Relationships can take a huge toll on a teen's well-being. Romance and falling in love are often rollercoaster experiences with sharp ups and downs. It's not uncommon for teens to quickly get in and out of relationships. For some, it's no big deal. But for others, the impact of a break-up can be devastating. Amid the process of awkward flirting, strong feelings, and endless crushes—exists the risk of many broken hearts. As a teen, you may have already experienced the hurt resulting from love and break-ups. Sometimes relationships end due to a lack of time, attention, or commitment from one or both partners. Or, a couple may grow apart due to differences of opinion or a change of feelings. Other times, hurt might come from a love that was only "hoped" for. **Heartbreak** is the overwhelming feeling of grief, deep longing, and intense emotional pain resulting from an experience of love. Symptoms of heartbreak include sadness, anger, jealousy, emptiness, and a heavy heart. Heartbreak does not always have to be about a boyfriend or girlfriend. You might also suffer the end of a close friendship or the death of a loved one.

Some heartbreaks will last a few weeks, while others can last up to several months. Regardless of the circumstances, heartbreaks can lead to alarming outcomes such as a lack of sleep, obsessive thoughts, depression, and even self-harm. To understand the cause of your strong feelings, it's important to understand how your teen brain is wired to work. During adolescence, your brain is still in its early stages of development and has yet to require a consistent ability to rationalize emotions. For now, your brain is capable of thinking in a "here and now" context but struggles slightly with thinking in a "future" context. This is completely normal. Your brain will continue to develop and change as you grow into an adult. This scientific background is the key to understanding why the pain of a heartbreak may feel like it will last forever. Teens will have a more difficult time getting over an unrequited crush or a sour breakup than will adults. The profound impact of a love disillusionment may even trigger teens to question their *self-worth*.

But the reality is that your pain will not last forever and your "bad" experience is actually a great display of your maturity. Showing that you can deeply care for someone besides yourself is a sign of *empathy*—an important social skill that we will talk about later in this book. Embracing *adaptability* will help you bounce back from any type of heartbreak with confidence. Being adaptable means being able to roll with the punches and accept change for what it is. Staying stuck on an ended relationship can destroy you. An adaptable person will

know how to let go of harmful feelings and move on with optimism. The key to adaptability is learning how to view situations with neutrality. Don't take change personally. Become self-aware of when the intensity of your feelings does not match up to the reality of the situation. Whether a romantic relationship ended before you were ready, your crush didn't correspond you with the same feelings, or your favorite buddy decided to abandon the friendship—heartbreak is never easy. However, with the right amount of willpower, there are many ways to reduce the pain of a loss.

Reflect upon your feelings 💔 Part of the healing process is recognizing and validating your emotions. Your sadness or anger is not a sign of weakness—it's a sign of a healthy human being. It's OK to cry out your emotions after a heartbreak. Ignoring your feelings can actually make it more difficult to get over someone. Share your feelings with people you trust, such as your friends or family. Talking to a sympathetic ear can make you feel better, or at the very least—give you a good shoulder to cry on. You can also write out your feelings in a journal if you rather be more private with your woes.

Make a list of their flaws 💔 Oftentimes, your romantic feelings for someone can blind you from seeing them for who they truly are. You might believe they are the most amazing person to exist on the planet and that you will never find anyone else to replace them. You might ignore their less than favorable qualities, simply because you love them. However, idealizing your ex will only worsen and prolong your heartbreak. Think about everything you did not like about your ex. Write down a list of their worst habits, personality traits, and overall defects. For example, did they always forget to open the door for you? Listing out each flaw will help you realize that your ex was not perfect.

Eliminate reminders 💔 Keeping relationship mementos such as photos, love letters, or gifts will make it harder for you to move on. Delete old text conversations, pawn any jewelry gifts, donate any stuffed animals, and return all borrowed clothing back to your ex. Don't listen to any songs that remind you of your ex and abstain from revisiting any places where you spent special moments together. If you met any friends through your ex, avoid hanging out with them for a while. Temporarily cutting off social media can also speed up your recovery process. Unfollow, block, or delete your ex from your profiles and stop checking their social media posts. Don't reply to any new messages your ex might send.

Get busy again 💔 You had a life before your ex. So, why wouldn't you be able to resume your normal routine after a breakup? A little distraction can go a long way. Keep your schedule busy with your favorite hobbies, schoolwork, family time, chores, and by going out with your friends. Treat yourself to a movie, concert, sports game, a new haircut, or a full day of shopping. Doing something fun can help you ease the pain of a heartbreak. Most importantly, now is the time to take good care of yourself. Eat healthy foods, get enough sleep, and get active. Scientific studies show that exercising triggers the release of your brain's *endorphins*, which can help uplift your mood.[4] Go out into nature for a relaxing jog or walk.

Give yourself time 💔 Don't blame yourself for what happened and know that time heals all wounds. Resist the urge to find yourself a "rebound." Instead of quickly jumping into another relationship, give yourself some time to be single. Being alone can help you remember all the qualities that make you a great person. It's important to work through your wounded feelings before you seek out another romance. Any unresolved emotions you have for your ex can sabotage your future chances of having a healthy relationship. You might become unconsciously resentful of love or act bitter toward your future partner.

Relationships and break-ups can be one of the most traumatic events for teens. But relationships are also one of the most rewarding learning experiences of our youth. Sometimes, we learn the most about ourselves from heartbreaks than from relationships that were "easy" or "comfortable." It is from each break-up that we can develop the healthy relationship skills we'll need to later find our "forever partner."

---

[4] Correlation between exercise and stress relief according to Mayo Clinic.

Awkward Moment #4: Academic Breakdown

A teen's schedule is always busy. You're probably juggling school, sports, extracurricular activities, family, friends, a part-time job, and a relationship all at the same time. You're trying to get perfect grades while also dealing with a lot of social drama. And for those teens who are close to graduating, the pressure to get accepted into a university increases each year. Every time a new class graduates, the bar seems to rise just a little higher. You're probably worrying about your future and agonizing over who you'll become once you're "all grown up."

Add to this the high expectations your parents, teachers, and society have for you—and the stress of keeping up can lead you to a nervous breakdown. **Academic stress** is a recurrent but unfortunate part of adolescence. Teens often feel they are in a competition against classmates and even against time. The burden of being the best can quickly drown you into a pool of anxiety. According to a study performed by the American Psychological Association, 83 percent of teens identified academics as a "somewhat" or "significant" source of stress.[5]

Another 60 percent said having to manage too many activities at once, was also a "somewhat" or "significant" stressor. Today's clinicians are witnessing an evolving increase in the anxiety levels of teens. Our modern-day *"race to success"* culture has prompted teens to become worry-warts, over-achievers, and perfectionists. These traits can make it hard for teens to settle for grades that are only "good"—much less for those considered "average." The real harm occurs when teens begin placing more importance on the end result than on the actual process of learning. Signs of academic stress can show up through emotional, physical, behavioral, or cognitive reactions. You might experience agitation, paranoia, fatigue, depression, headaches, stomachaches, decreased concentration, forgetfulness, insomnia, or a change in eating habits. Stress can also weaken your immune system—making you more susceptible to getting sick. Teens who are on the verge of an academic breakdown report feeling like they are "falling apart." Becoming overwhelmed by schoolwork can also lead to other problems such as test anxiety.

Test anxiety is the nervous feeling some people get on the day of a test. Teens who struggle with test anxiety might "blank out, freeze up, [or] zone out" right before starting a test. You might find it difficult to "get it together" and "respond to those questions you knew the answers to [the night before]."[6] If you are always stressed and notice you frequently experience breakdowns, it may be time to change your habits. Realize it's

---

[5] *"Are Teens Adopting Adults' Stress Habits?"* study performed by the American Psychological Association.
[6] Characteristics of *test anxiety* according to TeensHealth from Nemours.

impossible to check everything off your list. Saying yes to one commitment may force you to say no to another. You won't always be able to please your parent, teacher, coach, friend, or significant other—and that's OK. Aim for a *balanced* life in which you can productively separate the *important* tasks from those that are *optional*. In other words, learn to prioritize. Too *much* or too *little* of something will negatively affect your schedule, but just the *right* amount can lead you to success. For example, multitasking is a sign that you're doing too much, whereas boredom is a sign that you're doing too little. Practice moderation across all your activities and keep your expectations in-check. ***Time management***, ***organization***, and ***goal-setting*** can help you prevent future academic breakdowns with confidence.

Eliminate procrastination 📕 Resist the urge to put off work until the last minute. You'll only end up working twice as hard and become frantic. Instead, be prepared and get a head start on any studying, required readings, and assignments. Most teachers give students plenty of notice for upcoming tests and projects. Know your deadlines and plan accordingly. You don't have to wait until you get home to start studying. Good studying starts with note-taking in the classroom. Write down facts and anything your teacher writes on the board. If you get intimidated by large projects, try chunking. *"Chunking"* is the process of breaking big tasks into smaller, more manageable parts. For example, you can make writing an essay easier by separating it into introduction, body, conclusion, works cited, etc.—and only work on one section at a time. One last tip is to prepare for school the night before. Pack your lunch, pick out your clothes, and organize your backpack so you can still have time for breakfast in the morning.

Utilize resources 📕 There are many tools out there that can help you organize your time and remind you of all due dates. Once you have your tasks recorded, it will be hard to forget them. You can use an agenda planner, make to-do lists, set up calendar alerts through your phone, or use any productive app of your choice. These tools not only help you keep track of assignments, but also of your sports practices, doctors' appointments, and social events. Mapping out your weeks will help you conveniently distribute your workload. Plan out the amount of time you will dedicate to different tasks based on their priority. For example, you can set aside 30 minutes each Wednesday to study for a short quiz but reserve two hours every Monday to study for a big exam.

Organize your stuff 📕 Being disorderly can result in more academic stress. Spending hours searching for a misplaced item means less time studying. Use binders, notebooks, or folders to keep your documents organized by subject. Don't forget to regularly clean out your backpack and school locker. Throw away the things you no longer need and store any remaining class materials in a safe place. If you are constantly losing your papers and USBs, or are scared that your computer might spontaneously crash—consider using Google Docs to keep your assignments secure. Google Docs is a Gmail feature that saves your work in real-time and allows you to access it through any device with an internet connection.

Designate a workspace 🎒 Establish a space that will only be used for academic work. This could be a study room, an office, a library—or anywhere else with a table or desk. Just make sure this place is quiet enough for you to concentrate, and open enough for you to spread out all your work. Some people will like listening to classical music while studying, while others will prefer complete silence. However, you should generally avoid working in loud, distracting environments. As soon as you sit down, your brain should be able to focus quickly and recognize that it's there to work. This is why it's probably not a good idea to study in a place such as your bed. You'll either become too sleepy to study or your brain will learn to become hyperalert during your bedtime.

Set up SMART goals 🎒 Goals that work the best are *Specific, Measurable, Attainable, Relevant*, and *Timely*. "I'm going to get an "A" on my math exam by studying for an hour five days a week until September 12th," is a much more doable goal than "I'm going to ace my test." Moreover, repeating your goal can make it easier for you to stick to it. State your goal out loud or write it down to remind yourself of what you're working for. Set your goals into small steps and give yourself credit each time you accomplish one.

Consider a study group 🎒 Consider joining or starting a study group if you are feeling stressed about an upcoming test. Study groups can provide you with the extra practice needed to master a tricky subject. Students who are taking the same test can come together and use their unique strengths to counteract each other's weaknesses. You can help one another review material, confirm accuracy of notes, and come up with creative ways to remember concepts. If you find group work distracting, it may be more beneficial for you to receive one-on-one tutoring with a subject expert.

Know your boundaries 🎒 Everyone has a limit. Learn to speak up when you have reached yours. If you suddenly realize you're in over your head and have over-committed, don't be afraid to ask for help. Most individuals have no problem being flexible as long as you are respectful, honest, and clear about what you have done, can do, and will do. Request an extension from your teacher, coach, or boss. Also, remember to take short breaks between studying to avoid burnout. Get up from your desk, stretch, and walk around to refresh your mind and stay focused.

Academic stress can be one of your biggest downfalls as a teen. But if you change your habits you will be more confident, relaxed, and will perform better in school. Learn to view your mistakes as *learning opportunities* and not as failures. Instead of always trying to be No.1, focus on your efforts and improvements. Your learning progress is more important than achieving perfection. Don't beat yourself up over small slip-ups. Lastly, remember to be *present*. The majority of academic stress comes from "what if..." thoughts, instead of reality. Limit discussions and thoughts about the future and start living in the moment.

Awkward Moment #5: Catfishing 😮

The invention of new technologies and the internet has brought a vast amount of improvements to our lives. For one, we can now communicate faster. We no longer have to rely on post offices to mail letters back and forth. Secondly, we can now connect with millions of people across the world at the touch of a fingertip. We are no longer restricted by geographical boundaries. For teenagers, these new inventions have even more value because they've never lived without them. **Social media** is "a form of electronic communication through which users create online communities to share information, ideas, personal messages, and other content (like videos)."[7] Platforms such as Instagram, Snapchat, Facebook, and Twitter have become such necessary parts of a teen's routine—that most cannot imagine a world without them. As a teen, you were born and raised alongside social media and view it with the same naturalness as the air you breathe. But you may be surprised to realize that social media is actually a fairly new phenomenon. It wasn't too long ago that social media was born.

The earliest version of social media appeared in 1997 but most of the platforms teenagers know today are 21st century creations. For example, YouTube came out in 2005, Facebook and Twitter in 2006, Instagram in 2010, and Snapchat—the "baby" of all trending platforms—in 2011.[8] And there are no signs social media's

---
[7] Definition of *social media* according to the Merriam-Webster dictionary.
[8] Timeline of *social media* evolution according to History Cooperative.

evolution will be stopping. In the future, we can expect the release of new platforms that will either completely replace or at least directly compete with the ones we currently use. Social media will continue to enrich our lives for a very long time. However, social media's relatively new existence also raises important questions and issues worth examining. How is social media affecting the lives of today's teenagers? It's true that social media has and will continue to provide teens with *opportunities*, but has social media also brought along *problems*? On its own, social media is not a bad thing. In fact, it's a great way for teens to stay in touch with friends, family, and the world. But when used for the wrong reasons, social media can quickly transform into a double-edged sword.

Today's teens are exposed to many dangers their parents, grandparents, and other adults never had to face in their adolescence. *Catfishing* is a slang term for the act of setting up a fake personal profile on social media to use as a tool of deception. A *catfish* will go online and pretend to be someone they're not by using strangers' photos as their own. Think of catfish as invasive creatures that contaminate the ocean (our internet) with deception. A once, healthy ecosystem (our social media) can quickly become polluted and generate consequences for all those who inhabit it. Facebook is a living testimony of this plague. In 2008 alone, the social media giant worked vigorously to remove 1.2 billion fake accounts from its platform.[9] You've probably been *catfished* if you were trolled or tricked into an online relationship by a false identity. You may have never suspected the "gorgeous model" or "undercover celebrity" you were chatting with, was actually an online criminal. Teens are especially vulnerable to online predators who like to use social media for sinister motives. They are more likely to accept friend requests from strangers and overshare intimate information about their emotions or life.

For example, being vocal about wanting a relationship might encourage a pedophile to disguise themselves as your next teen boyfriend or girlfriend. There are several reasons why someone might create a fake persona online. Sometimes, catfish are just lonely individuals who search for romance, excitement, an emotional thrill, or anything else they lack in their real lives. Other times, catfish are professional scammers who use deception to commit identity theft or financial fraud. And in the most extreme cases, catfish will create fake profiles to sexually assault, kidnap, or murder their targets. Regardless of the motives, catfishing is never a pleasant experience. The victims end up investing an infinite amount of time, energy—and sometimes even money—into a false relationship. Falling into these traps can make you feel shocked, betrayed, embarrassed, disheartened, robbed, and horrified. So, how can you avoid the dangerous facets of social media? *Safe social networking skills* will help you prevent online deception with confidence. Catching a catfish is just a matter of using a little common sense and being hyperaware of each warning sign.

---

[9] Facebook's report of fake account-removal for 2008 according to Vox.

They have new or incomplete profiles ⚠ You can spot a catfish by taking a close look at their social media profiles. Profiles with few or no followers/friends are usually fake. Or, you might notice that the user's online connections are of only one age and gender. For example, a male catfish might have a large ratio of teenage girls as his "friends." Profiles with only one or few photos are also suspicious. A catfish might use the same photo year after year and never appear to age. Also, examine the user's social media activity. If the user has little to no social interactions, their profile may be fake. Catfish post sparingly, have few likes, and are not tagged in any photos. And if the user created their profile just days before you met, you should be extra suspicious.

They seem too good to be true ⚠ Catfish like to create flawless, fake profiles to appear more attractive than they actually are. Are they remarkably beautiful, handsome, or perfect in all their photos? Do their photos look like they have been photoshopped, retouched, or airbrushed? Be wary of extremely professional photos. Many catfish will claim to be models, celebrities, or actors by stealing photos off the internet. *Real* people typically use photos snapped by their smartphones—not glamour shots. Furthermore, catfish usually have "interests" that are broad enough to match with those of anyone else. What you think might be a common interest (listening to music) that brings you two together—may actually be a premeditated tactic of manipulation. Remember—if something seems too good to be true, it's probably not real.

They have a lot of writing errors ⚠ A catfish might claim they're from the same country as you, but show poor command of your native language through their writing. Abbreviations, acronyms, shortcuts, and "text" language compromise the majority of our online communication. In a moment of rush, we might make a spelling error, misplace a comma, or forget to punctuate the end of our sentences. It's normal for everyone to have minor typos every now and then. However, if you notice *too* many language errors within *every* message your suspect sends—it's probably not a coincidence. Catfish are notorious for bad grammar and sentence structure.

The relationship progresses quickly ⚠ If you recently met someone on social media and the conversation becomes quickly romantic, you may have a catfish on your hands. Catfish like to create romantic bonds with their potential victims usually within days or weeks of meeting. They will pretend to develop strong feelings within the first few exchanges, in order to push a relationship forward. What begins as casual flirtation might rapidly turn into undying declarations of love, passionate love letters, or even marriage proposals. Although it may feel good to receive over-the-top attention, you should never trust people who say "I love you" to someone they've never met in real life. Your new online friend may just be trying to manipulate you.

They request money ⚠ People typically ask for help from someone they have known for a long time, such as a family member or a friend. However, it's highly unusual for people to ask for help from a stranger on the web. If an online friend is asking you for money, you may be dealing with a catfish. Catfish always seem to need help. They make up stories of losing their job, being unable to pay their internet bill, or of their car breaking down. Catfish might request expensive gifts, wire transfers, gift cards, money orders, or cashier's checks. And if you hesitate or refuse to send any funds, they will try to make you feel guilty. Remember—catfish are expert manipulators.

They avoid personal communication ⚠ Let's say you've been chatting with an online friend for a while and you're ready to take the relationship to the next level. You might request a live meeting through webcam/video chat or suggest a real-time talk on the phone. But every time you make plans to meet on Facetime or Skype, your friend always bails at the last minute. Catfish are well-known for strictly limiting their communication to online, *written* messaging. They conveniently dodge personal meetings with excuses such as "internet connection issues," or other last-minute emergencies. Catfish avoid revealing their face and voice because they know it'll blow their cover and expose their true identities. In other cases, a catfish will agree to meet you in-person but only in a secluded, private place where the two of you will be completely alone. These catfish are extremely dangerous, as they will try to physically hurt you.

They have elaborate stories ⚠ You can spot a catfish by paying close attention to their communication. Catfish are notorious for living exceptionally "unusual" lives. They have a habit of using outlandish stories, excuses, and explanations to deceive you. They will pull on your heartstrings by sharing intimate stories of childhood trauma, or of other similar struggles. They might also try to gain your pity by claiming they've been diagnosed with a cancer, or with another similar illness. Their goal is to make a quick emotional connection with you. Another common tale catfish like to tell is about having a "job" that takes them all around the globe. They will use their constant "travel" as an excuse for not having a permanent address. Some catfish will even claim to be "stuck" in a foreign country in order to get your money. Other times, catfish will lie about being extremely "wealthy." Watch out for answers like, "I'm a billionaire who runs my own business" or "I'm a photographer who makes a ton of money."

It's always fishing season on the internet. Be aware of stranger-danger online. Don't let your guard down and watch out for catfish before they bite. Online photos and messages are not enough to fully know someone. Be careful of who you befriend. Take your time in forming connections through social media and never agree to meet someone alone. If you're pursuing an online relationship and notice any red flags, do something! You can easily perform a Google image search on the suspect's photos to see if they were stolen. Additionally, you can use the website, *SocialCatfish*, to  investigate the legitimacy of users' social media profiles. Report phony profiles to their respective social media provider and block any suspicious users. You know the saying—"It's better to be safe than sorry."

Awkward Moment #6: Bullying

Bullying is "a form of aggressive behavior in which someone intentionally and repeatedly causes another person injury or discomfort."[10] This aggressive behavior is usually triggered by a real or perceived imbalance of power. Bullying can occur anywhere from your school, to the workplace, to your neighborhood, and even over the internet. The majority of bullies are self-absorbed people who lack proper social skills. They have difficulty processing normal emotions such as empathy, compassion, guilt, or remorse and have trouble getting along with others. Bullies like to hurt people's feelings because it gives them a sense of control. They often bully others for **power, popularity, payback, problems, pleasure, prejudice,** or **peer pressure**—the seven "P's."[11] For example, some teens do it for mere attention or amusement, while others do it to fit in with a clique or gain social status. Or, they might do it to make fun of someone who is different—such as a teen with a learning disability. Teens will also use bullying to get revenge on someone they feel "did them wrong."

Bullies pretend to be tough and act like they don't care. But behind the facade, hides an insecure individual who is really just trying to make themselves feel better. In fact, bullying is frequently used as a *coping mechanism* by teens who come from problematic households. Risk factors for becoming a bully include

---
[10] Definition of *bullying* according to the American Psychological Association.
[11] Reasons for bullying according to Verywell Family.

witnessing violence in the home, being the victim of abuse or neglect, having siblings who are bullies, or having emotionally detached parents. Whatever the case may be, the bully is trying to meet a need in a dysfunctional manner. Some bullies will be outgoing and aggressive, while others will be sneaky and quiet. However, the most common types of bullies are those who you least expect—people who are friendly but fake. These people are often referred to as "frenemies." If you think you have never been a perpetuator or a victim of bullying, you may want to think again. The stereotypical portrayal of the classroom jock beating up the classroom nerd is not the only situation in which bullying takes place.

Apart from being **physical**, bullying can also be **verbal**, **emotional**, **social**, **psychological**, or **cyber**. You're probably aware that teasing, name-calling, pushing, and hitting are key features of bullying. But did you know *gossip* also constitutes as bullying? Spreading rumors to intentionally damage someone's reputation is a covert form of *social* bullying. Similarly, excluding an individual from a group on purpose, is a form of *psychological* bullying. Teens are often guilty of this type of bullying when they convince their peers not to be friends with someone they don't like. Emotions such as jealousy, anger, and fear are usually at the root of these hurtful acts. In other cases, bullying occurs via electronic technology such as social networking sites, chat rooms, email, instant messaging, or texts. Four out of every five high school students say they have been cyberbullied.[12] A bully might use the internet to anonymously write mean messages, share embarrassing photos or videos, make threats, or to hack an enemy's online account.

Additionally, bullying can take place in the form of stalking or sexual harassment. Teen girls are especially vulnerable to this type of bullying when guys take flirtation to the extreme with inappropriate touching, suggestive gestures, or by making comments of a sexual nature. If you've been a target of bullying, you may have been picked on for your appearance, behavior, race, religion, social status, or sexual identity. Bullying has the potential to scar some teens for life. Victims will often feel afraid, stressed, depressed, lonely, confused, ashamed, or anxious and experience a loss of control. Their academic performance might also suffer in the form of slipping grades and increased absenteeism. The all-consuming impact of bullying may even compel a teen to drop out of school. Bullying can have long-term consequences for all parties involved. It can later lead to more serious problems such as violence, trust issues, drug and alcohol abuse, post-traumatic stress disorder, self-harm, or suicide. So, whether you're the abuser or the victim—it's important to know how to stop this malicious situation. **Assertiveness**, *empathy*, and **conflict resolution** will help you overcome bullying with confidence.

---

[12] Statistical ratio of teen cyberbullying according to LearnPsychology.

Confront the bully 🔑 Assertive teens are neither passive nor aggressive. They defend themselves in a respectful manner without the use of violence. Speak up when you don't like the way you are being treated. Maintaining strong eye contact, walking tall, and holding your head high will show the bully that you are not vulnerable. Point out the bully's behavior, ask why they do it, and then explain how their actions are harmful to you. For example, you might say, "I notice you say mean things about me anytime I leave a room. What are your reasons for talking behind my back? Are you aware that it makes me feel disrespected?" Use a calm and clear voice to work out a solution. You can also stand up for friends or others who are being bullied. The key to peaceful conflict resolution is asking questions, listening to others' opinions, and expressing your own needs and wants with honesty.

Ask for help 🔑 You don't always have to know the answers or handle an issue on your own to be a successful conflict-resolver. Part of being an assertive teen is knowing when to ask for help. Too many bullying victims make the mistake of staying quiet. Ignoring a problem does not make it go away. Reach out to an adult you trust such as a parent, teacher, coach, or a guidance counselor. Authority figures can often address bullying without having to tell the bully how they found out or without revealing who reported them. Talking to someone can give you the support, resources, and strategies needed to overcome bullying. Never feel ashamed to reveal your fears and frustrations. You have a right to seek help and are entitled to safety. According to anti-bullying expert, Jonathan Fast,

> "It is not the victim's responsibility to protect themselves in school; it is the duty of the school to create a non-hostile atmosphere where students do not have to worry about hurt or humiliation and can concentrate on the learning."[13]

Collect evidence 🔑 If you are being cyberbullied, it is important you collect any evidence of the scandal. Make copies of all the bully's communications. Take screenshots, save text messages, and print out emails so you have proof something fraudulent occurred. Cyberbullying can be reported to the relevant online service provider or to the social media safety center. Review the terms of service and identify which of the agreement's clauses were violated by the bully's behavior. Additionally, you can report cyberbullying to your school if it was committed by a classmate. Most states require schools to have a cyberbullying policy in place. Once bullying progresses into a crime, you should immediately report it to the correct authorities. Cyberbullying may involve an invasion of privacy, stalking, hate crimes, child pornography, financial fraud, or threats of violence. In these cases, you will need to report it to law enforcement. The same goes for bullying that involves physical or sexual assault—collect proof of the harassment and report it to the police.

---

[13] Quote from Jonathan Fast, Associate professor at Wurzeiler School of Social Work of Yeshiva University, on LearnPsychology.

Practice kindness 🔑 Teens can prevent bullying by learning how to relate to one another. **Empathy** is the "experience of understanding another person's thoughts, feelings, and condition from his or her point of view, rather than from one's own."[14] In other words, empathy is all about putting yourself in someone else's shoes or "treating others the way you want to be treated." If you're a bully, imagine how you would feel if you were the target. How would you react if someone called you "dumb" or "ugly"? Would you like going to school if you were constantly pushed around in the hallways or harassed in the courtyard? Empathy keeps us from hurting others and is the key to forming close relationships. Similarly, it is important for teens to be respectful of their peers' backgrounds, such as religion or race. Many teens will bully others who they perceive as "inferior" or "different." Being *tolerant* can help you accept differing points of views, appreciate diversity, and help you recognize the similarities you share with others.

Join a bullying prevention program 🔑 Peer mediation is a great tool for both the bully and the one being bullied. These group-based programs have been effectively proven to reduce bullying among teenagers. The victim and the bully get the opportunity to share their experiences in an environment that is both safe and nonjudgmental. They receive tips and advice according to their personal situations, and usually make an anti-bullying pledge as part of the program. Consider joining **PACER's National Bullying Prevention Center, The Olweus Bullying Prevention Program,** or **StopBullying.gov**. Alternatively, bullies can decide to join a social-emotional learning program that specializes in teaching empathy.

Bullying can easily manifest itself into a vicious cycle of low self-esteem. In the beginning, low self-esteem will trigger a bully to lash out on others. Next, the bullying will cause an otherwise secure teenager, to become a victim of low self-esteem. Lastly, the victim may then become bitter and choose to turn into a bully themselves—therefore repeating the process. It's not easy ending the bullying cycle. But with the right amount of strength and confidence, you can be the first person to break the chain. You don't have to be another piece of the trauma. Every teen has the ability to change and make the world a better place. Victims of bullying should consider getting therapy to reduce its negative effects. Never play with your life. If you're feeling hopeless, immediately reach out to a suicide hotline for help.

---

[14] Definition of *empathy* according to Psychology Today.

Awkward Moment #7: Body Image

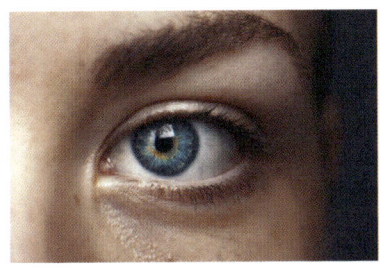

With the arrival of adolescence, comes the much dreaded but long-awaited introduction of puberty. As you slowly transition from child to adult, you will go through various physical changes that will make it difficult to recognize and accept your teenage body. A combination of unpredictable hormones, acne, braces, and awkward haircuts can all contribute to a challenging adjustment. You may suddenly start to become hyperaware of every blemish, every pound, or every movement you make. Or, you might begin worrying about being too short, too tall, too thin, too fat, or even too "average." Every teen will have their own personal insecurity. Some teens will begin to gain weight—becoming thicker or curvier—despite their persistent efforts to exercise regularly and eat healthy foods. Other teens will struggle to "fill out" their clothes—staying lean or skinny—despite binging on junk food or skipping out on workouts. Whereas some teens will feel self-conscious about their accelerated growth spurt, others will feel self-conscious about being a "late-bloomer." Regardless of the differences, every teen's confidence will falter at various points throughout their adolescence.

Eventually, all teens come to ask themselves the same question—"Is this really my body?!" ***Body image*** is the subjective interpretation you have of your body "when you look in the mirror or…picture yourself in your mind." Body image includes your beliefs about your appearance (your assumptions, generalizations, and memories), your feelings toward your body shape (weight, height, etc.), and how you physically experience your body (your sense of control over movements).[15] Note that body image is not an accurate representation of what your body looks like in real life. It's merely an image constructed from your thoughts, feelings, and opinions. It's normal for everyone to have the desire to change at least one aspect of their body—whether it be the color of their eyes, the size of their nose, or the presence of a birthmark. However, an individual with a ***positive body image*** will accept their body without dwelling on perceived flaws. According to psychology professional, Ondina Hatvany, a "healthy body image means you are comfortable with the body you have. It does not mean you think your body is perfect, rather, that you accept it and commit to loving and caring for it."[16]

On the other hand, an individual with a ***negative body image*** will remain preoccupied with their perceived flaws. They will feel repulsion or shame toward their appearance and will try to modify or conceal their bodies. That being said, body image is generally not a static factor. Your attitude toward your body will change as you become exposed to new experiences, information, or people. Throughout adolescence, you will switch back and forth between negative and positive feelings. A teen's body image will be influenced by

---

[15] Definiton of *body image* according to the National Eating Disorders Association.
[16] Quote obtained from "Body Image," GoodTherapy.

several social factors such as cultural background, interactions with family and friends, and the media. **Media** is the main means of mass communication and includes channels such as television, magazines, and the internet. Advertisements and social media posts from "influencers" can all have a strong effect on teens' perceptions of their bodies. The media often depicts an unrealistic and unattainable standard of beauty with picture-perfect people. Hatvany notes, "You only have to turn the TV on for five minutes to hear the message that if we look a certain way, we too can have that stellar-looking partner hanging off our arm or that perfect dream job. In fact, all we have to do is buy the advertised shampoo, get the right hair, attain the correct weight, and all the love, success, and glory we desire will follow!"[17]

These messages are extremely harmful to teens, as most are still learning how to be comfortable in their own skin. Body dissatisfaction has also been linked to social media usage. It's not uncommon for teens to compare their average life moments with another person's "best" social media moments. They disproportionately compare their everyday "unfiltered" appearance with the flattering and flawless photos of social media. Over 80 percent of American women are dissatisfied with their bodies, while around 34 percent of men suffer from negative body image.[18] Although the media has had a bigger impact on women, the "ideal" male body portrayed by ads has still had a considerable effect on men. A teen's desire to be "pretty" or "attractive" can quickly turn into a dangerous obsession for both genders.

Body dysmorphia (BDD) is an extreme form of body image distortion in which a person becomes obsessed with body parts they believe are flawed. People with BDD partake in compulsive behaviors such as "excessive grooming, skin-picking, double-checking their appearance in the mirror, and seeking reassurance from others about their looks."[19] Other mental and physical disorders include muscle, dysmorphia, anorexia, and bulimia. Teen girls might develop an eating disorder, while teen boys might develop an addiction to getting more muscular. It can be hard to value our bodies when the media repeatedly sends us the message that we are not "good enough." However, it's important for teens to adapt healthy habits to appreciate and take care of their bodies. Practicing **self-acceptance** and **self-compassion** will help you adjust to your growing body with confidence.

---

[17] Quote obtained from "Body Image," GoodTherapy.
[18] Correlation between body image and gender according to GoodTherapy.
[19] Definition of *Body Dysmorphic Disorder* according to Good Therapy.

Realize you're not alone 💪 Sometimes, it's easy for teens to get stuck on themselves and forget about the rest of the world. If you often catch yourself saying, "I'm the only one who…"—it may be time for a wake-up call. Seventy-three percent of teens agree their appearance affects their body image. Fifty percent of teens are "self-conscious" about their bodies. Sixty-five percent of teens are afraid of gaining weight. [20] You are not the only one suffering from body image issues. Your emotions are shared and universal. Your friend, your classmate, your next-door neighbor and your sister are all dealing with similar issues. Everyone is too preoccupied with themselves to actually realize that nobody is judging them.

Embrace what makes you unique 💪 Imagine what the world would be like if everyone looked the same. Needless to say—it would be pretty boring. But even if all teens began exercising the same amount and began eating the same foods for an entire year, they still would not look alike by the end of that year. This is because every teen's body shape and bone structure will depend on his or her genetic background and cultural traits. Striving to look like somebody else is not only impossible, but also miserable. Don't compare yourself to others. Your body features are not inferior to another's. Your differences are your strengths, not your weaknesses. Beauty is subjective, not objective. Nobody is perfect, but everyone *is* special. Be grateful for who you are. You never know—someone might be secretly wishing they had one of *your* unique characteristics.

Accept your body 💪 Identify any features you like about your body. Is it your curly hair, your heart-shaped face, your slender hands, the tone of your shoulders, or the color of your eyes? It might even be the color of your lips or the shape of your collarbone. If you have trouble thinking of something, ask your friends or family. What do they always compliment you on? Next, make a list of your top ten features and read it regularly. Continue adding to the list as you discover more things you like about yourself. Lastly, appreciate your body for what it can *do*, not just for how it looks. Celebrate all the incredible things your body can accomplish. It's there for you every time you need to breathe, laugh, stretch, reach, walk, run, climb, or jump. Without your body, you wouldn't be able to carry things, make your breakfast, or drive a car. Your body gives you autonomy. Write down another list of your body's strengths. For example, do your legs allow you to play a sport? Do your hands let you play music or create art? These exercises are called **body image boosters** because they help you feel good about yourself.

---

[20] Teen body image statistics according to the National Organization for Women.

Use positive self-talk 💪 Do you constantly body-shame yourself? Making harsh comments about how you look—whether out loud or in your head—can negatively affect your self-esteem. *Positive self-talk* is the practice of replacing your self-criticism with self-praise. It's the act of overpowering your negative thoughts with positive ones. For example, the next time you hear yourself saying, "*I hate my body,*" replace it by saying "*I'm beautiful inside and out.*" Try complimenting yourself every day. Speak to yourself with the same kindness you would use with a best friend that is struggling with body image. Be your body's best fan, not its worst critic.

Focus on what you *can* control 💪 A negative body image can make you feel powerless. Learn to let go of the things you can't change. Instead of wishing you had someone else's straight smile, trim waist, lean legs, tall height, or light skin color—focus your time and energy on the things you *can* change. Start by exercising for your *health* and not for your *weight*. You can choose any physical activity you enjoy such as swimming, yoga, or dancing. Next, focus on eating *healthy* instead of *dieting*. Eat when you're hungry and stop when you're full. Take the time to taste your food. Lastly, wear clothes that you feel good in. The right fit is neither baggy nor tight. Buy yourself a few wardrobe pieces that will make you feel more confident such as a nice necklace, a cool T-shirt, or some trendy shoes.

Use media wisely 💪 Be picky with your media use and only choose channels that reflect your values and boost your body image. If necessary, limit the time you spend looking at content with perfect-body images. Studies show that the more exposed we are to media, the more likely we are to compare our self-image with unrealistic body standards. Filter your media by quality and quantity. Start off by monitoring your social media usage. For example, instead of checking Instagram every day, schedule two days out of the week to use it for only 30 minutes. Learn to be critical of the messages you see in the media. Pay attention to images, slogans, or attitudes and ask yourself, "What is the message suggesting?" "Why is it being sent? Who is the target audience? Who is making the profits? Are the bodies real or digitally altered? Realize that celebrities, models, and actors usually have a whole entourage of fitness trainers, makeup artists, fashion stylists, plastic surgeons, dieticians, and publicists that help them look good. Even your friends' social media photos go through a lot of prep work. They might use photo editing apps or filters to get their posts looking flawless. Lastly, use your body image critiques to protest a negative media message. Express your concerns to the advertiser via a letter, email, or social media comment. You can even make a petition against the advertiser or choose to boycott its products.

Build a support system 💪 The people you spend the majority of your time with can have a huge impact on how you view yourself. *Energy* is contagious. The more you hang out with negative influences, the more likely you will become negative, yourself. Make it a habit to only surround yourself with *positive* people. If you have friends who constantly criticize your body or their own—consider getting new friends. Or, at the very least, try talking to your friends about their negative comments. The same goes for you. Do and say things that echo a confident body image. Give positive compliments to your friends. You can also support one another as workout buddies or as nutrition coaches. For example, you can start a running group or reserve a day to cook healthy meals together. The point is to *build* each other up.

Every teen deserves the right to feel healthy, confident, accepted, and beautiful for who they truly are. "True beauty" is not just a state of your body. Real beauty is a *state of the mind*. Many teens will often say, "I'll like my body once I get in better shape." Unfortunately, positive body image never works this way. You have to start loving yourself the way you are now. Learn to look at yourself as a whole person, instead of as an assembly of body parts. Be proud of the qualities that aren't related to your appearance. When you focus on aspects such as your personality, your intelligence, your talents, your morals, or your work ethic—your self-esteem is  less likely to be vulnerable and collapse. Love yourself and be patient with your body as it grows.

Awkward Moment #8: Isolation

Isolation is the experience of being separated from others by either chance or choice. Isolation may occur through various forms—it can be **physical**, **social**, or **emotional**. A person who is *physically* isolated is separated by geographical boundaries. These individuals usually live in remote places where it is difficult to find other people to interact with. For example, they might reside in the countryside, on a large acre that separates them from neighbors, or in an area that has limited internet connection—or none at all. People who live in cities and other highly populated areas are less likely to experience physical isolation. Social isolation is the unhealthy absence of social interactions. A person who is *socially* isolated will lack important social or professional relationships.[21] This type of isolation should not be confused with ***solitude***, which is simply the state of being alone. Solitude is often a temporary and healthy way to be alone, whereas social isolation is an extended and harmful experience of being lonely. Whereas solitude is usually a choice, social isolation is sometimes a form of forced peer rejection—such as in the case of bullying.

Other times, social isolation is a self-imposed situation triggered by ***social anxiety*** or ***depression***. A person might avoid social interactions due to shame or a fear of abandonment, despite their desire to form a part of society. A person who is *emotionally* isolated is "unable or unwilling to share their emotions with others." These individuals are usually withdrawn and "may be reluctant to discuss anything but the most superficial matters."[22] A person might become emotionally isolated as a side-effect of social isolation. However, emotional isolation can still occur to people who have a healthy social network. For example, emotional isolation can occur to someone in a relationship, despite having a boyfriend or girlfriend. Trust issues, abuse, or infidelity may cause one or both partners to feel alone instead of emotionally supported and fulfilled.[23] For some individuals, the mere act of "bonding" can be enough to trigger negative feelings or thoughts. These people will experience severe distress and anxiety when trying to emotionally connect with others. As a result, they will use emotional isolation as a defense mechanism. They might limit contact with their social network or completely withdraw from relationships in order to protect themselves. People with emotional isolation often report feeling "numb" or "shut-down."

Spending time away from others is not always a bad thing. In fact, it is completely normal for everyone to need some alone time every now and then, to recharge their energy. However, being alone becomes dangerous when a person's solitude transforms into a permanent state of loneliness. People who are lonely

---

[21] Characteristics of *social isolation* according to GoodTherapy.
[22] Definition of *emotional isolation* according to GoodTherapy.
[23] Characteristics of *emotional isolation* according to GoodTherapy.

will experience feelings of sadness and emptiness. They crave social contact but are unable to pursue it due to a state of isolation. Forty-seven percent of Americans do not have "meaningful in-person social interactions (such as quality time with family) on a daily basis."[24] Research shows there is a significant correlation between an individual's age and gender and their level of loneliness. According to a 2018 Cigna survey, the most vulnerable age groups to experience isolation are teenagers, young adults, and people over the age of 45. The survey identified Generation Z (adults ages 18-22) as the loneliest generation of our present-day.[25] Moreover, the study found men are more isolated than women, although they are less likely to admit feeling lonely. **Societal factors** may play a part in this discrepancy. For example, societies that emphasize masculinity (such as western cultures) may discourage men from revealing their emotions or from forming friendships with other men—out of fear of appearing homosexual.

Other **cultural factors** that play a role in isolation are not so gender-specific. The overall culture of a person's country of residence will have an equal effect on men and women's likeliness to become isolated. For example, people who live in countries that value *individualistic culture* (such as those who live in the U.S.), are more likely to report feeling lonely. On the other hand, those who live in countries that value *collectivist culture* (such as those who live in Italy), are less likely to report feeling lonely. Isolation can have various physical and mental consequences for a person's health. Physically, isolation can lead to the development of high blood pressure, coronary artery disease, higher levels of stress hormones, or Type 2 diabetes. Mentally, isolation can result in the development of depression, dementia, social anxiety, insomnia, and posttraumatic stress disorder. Isolation is often a very dehumanizing experience. Those who suffer from isolation as a youth, are advised to combat it immediately. Otherwise, isolation will continue to affect them as they become adults. It is absolutely crucial for teens to maintain connections and relationships with others, throughout their adolescence. Effective *interpersonal skills* can help you overcome isolation with confidence.

---

[24] Quoted statistic obtained from "Isolation," GoodTherapy.
[25] Research study quoted from "Age and Isolation," GoodTherapy.

Join an extracurricular activity ✅ Pursuing an interest or finding a hobby is a great way to form relationships and refine your interpersonal skills. For example, if you enjoy being active consider joining a sport. Don't worry about having to be a master athlete in order to begin. There's a sport for every person and their level of athleticism: swimming, dance, tennis, track and field, cycling, soccer, volleyball, basketball, football, martial arts, weightlifting, golf, gymnastics, etc. Working within a team will help you form close bonds with others and feel less lonely. Do you like snapping pictures? Join a photography club. Do you like reading? Join a book club. Are you interested in playing music? Join your school's band team. If you live in a physically isolating place, consider forming your community's first organization. Are you interested in travelling? Start your own travel club in your town! Or, you can consider becoming a member of your town's church. Every town—no matter how physically isolated it may be—will usually have a church.

Get a part-time job, an internship, or volunteer ✅ Pursuing a professional opportunity will help you overcome isolation and develop important skills you will need in the future. You will have the ability to list experience on your resume and the chance to meet plenty of new people. Apart from becoming life-long professional connections, your coworkers can also become life-long friends. People who work are often too busy to feel lonely. Obtain an after-school job at a local retail store, find an internship relevant to your future career interests, or volunteer for a cause you feel passionate about. For example, if you enjoy working with animals, consider volunteering at your local animal shelter. Or, if you dream of becoming a lawyer, consider applying as the office receptionist of a local law firm. Even working at a grocery store is helpful at combatting isolation.

Use social media to your advantage ✅ Social media can be a helpful or harmful way of dealing with isolation depending on the unique effect it has on each individual. For example, physically isolated individuals are very likely to benefit from the sense of community and belonging social media can provide. However, social media is harmful for individuals who use it to completely replace in-person connections. Superficial online interactions should not substitute meaningful, face-to-face conversations. And although social media was created as a form of connection—too much of it can make some users feel even lonelier. According to a 2017 study of adults aged 19 to 32, the most frequent social media users reported having "higher levels of perceived social isolation."[26] This study demonstrates the importance of *moderation*. You are less likely to feel isolated if you learn to use social media with restraint. The only time social media reduces isolation is when it fosters the creation of significant relationships. There are various apps such as ***Meetup*** or ***Bumble BFF*** that help you make new friends and find social events to attend based on your location. Use social media to organize in-person hangouts with your online friends.

---

[26] Research study quoted from "Does Social Media Cause Social Isolation?" GoodTherapy.

Prioritize family activities ✅ Bonding with your family members can significantly reduce loneliness. Although it is tempting to sacrifice your family time for an extra hour to complete school assignments or work—you may be doing yourself a huge disfavor. Your attempt at being more productive may actually be isolating you. Make it a priority to have dinner at the table with your family, at least five days a week. Enact a "no-cellphone" policy when you are with them. Moreover, try to attend every family get-together without a fault. This includes reunions, holidays, birthday parties, anniversaries, graduation ceremonies, and any other important celebrations. If you live away from any immediate or extended family members, make it a commitment to call or text one of them, every day. Being a *present* family member can help you understand the art of selfless "give-and-take." The relationship with your family can teach you how to be supportive and how to accept support—a very important interpersonal skill.

Reach out for therapy ✅ You don't have to deal with isolation on your own. If you feel your loneliness has become a threat to your health and safety—reach out to a professional therapist immediately. Therapy can help you improve your social connections in a setting that is both nonjudgmental and supportive. You and your therapist will work together to uncover the source of your loneliness and to discuss problem-solving strategies. For example, you may discover your isolation is due to a lack of social skills, feelings of superiority, or a fear of rejection. **Cognitive behavioral therapy (CBT)** and **exposure therapy** are effective ways of treating isolation. During CBT, "negative patterns of thought about the self and the world are challenged in order to alter unwanted behavior patterns or treat mood disorders."[27] During exposure therapy, "a person is gradually exposed to the situation that causes them distress…with the goal of reducing anxiety, decreasing avoidance of dreaded situations, and improving one's quality of life."[28] You can receive therapy both in-person and online.

Severe isolation can be catastrophic to a teen's health—and sometimes even life-threatening. Loneliness has the same effect on a teen's health as does smoking 15 cigarettes per day. Isolation increases your chances of developing a disability or chronic illness. Loneliness may even increase a person's risk of a premature death by 30 percent.[29] Human beings need social contact in order to survive and thrive. If you are suffering from any form of isolation, you can break free by enacting strong interpersonal skills in your everyday life.

---

[27] Definition of *cognitive behavioral therapy* according to the Oxford dictionary.
[28] Definition of *exposure therapy* according to GoodTherapy.
[29] Quoted statistic obtained from "Isolation," GoodTherapy.

Over to You 😀

"My times of being a teenager were short and are now officially over. But my memories are infinite, and my social learning process has only begun. Regrettably, I look back to realize I wasted a lot of valuable time focusing on my weaknesses instead of my strengths. I failed to look beyond my insecurities to recognize all the blessings I possessed. I was young, beautiful, and intelligent. It wasn't until I became an adult that I truly began to appreciate my journey as a teen. I often wonder how much more I would have enjoyed my adolescence if I had the same level of confidence I own today. Needless to say, I would have probably used my youth and time more wisely. Today, I want teens to know they have a choice. They can choose to start living their best life now, or they can choose to wait until they are adults."

Social skills are one of the most important skills teenagers can develop—as they are the key to building confidence and a predictor of future success. Research shows that "youth who score higher on social skill measurements are four times more likely to graduate from an undergraduate institution."[30] According to psychology professional, Monica Lake,

> *"Social skills [are] linked to job success, independence, and emotional well-being. Those with adaptive social skills often demonstrate superior ability to observe, problem solve, and respond in social situations."*[31]

This does not mean you have to be a "social butterfly" in order to develop social skills. Both **introverts** and **extroverts** have the same capacity to acquire healthy social skills. In fact, sometimes it is the most "outgoing" teens who have a harder time becoming socially adept, than those who are "reserved." Although extroverts may be good at making small talk, chatting with strangers, or speaking in public—they are not always good with **active listening**. Introverts, on the other hand, are usually great natural listeners. Despite their "quiet" demeanor, these teens typically demonstrate a remarkable level of social competence through their ability to empathize, observe and interpret body language, and understand social cues. Every teen will and *should* have their own unique personalities. Social skills are not about changing who you are. Social skills simply help you become the *best version* of yourself.

As a teen, you will be faced with various "awkward" situations on a daily basis. You will encounter peer pressure, stage fright, heartbreak, academic stress, social media dilemmas, bullying, body image issues, and maybe even some isolation—throughout your entire adolescence. And although we all wish we could eliminate

---

[30] Studies performed by Pennsylvania State University and Duke University.
[31] Quote obtained from "The Importance of Social Skills: Raising a Socially Intelligent Child" GoodTherapy.

these problems—they are impossible to evade. However, every teen has the capacity to survive and triumph over these problems with good social skills. Social skills are the armor that will help you win your teen battles with self-confidence. But their utility does not just end there. Social skills will continue helping you solve the challenges you'll face for the rest of your lifetime. Having poor social skills will significantly impact your ability to thrive as an adult. This is why it is extremely important for you to address the social learning process while you are still young. Don't wait for society, your school, or an adult to guide you through the social learning process. Unfortunately, they won't always be there to teach you or show you the correct answers. It will be your responsibility to find the right solutions to your problems, when no one is there to help you.

Developing effective social skills starts with being a good student. Never stop learning and growing. The most successful people are those who are teachable, humble, and hungry for knowledge. You must be willing to accept that no one is "above" or "better" than others. Accept constructive criticism without being defensive. Be trainable and ready to ask questions. Most importantly, don't be afraid of failure! Being fearless, taking risks, and failing repeatedly are all part of the path to success. Failure does not mean you have lost in the game of life. Our schools do not invest in the proper programs, skills, or strategies to teach youth how to accept failure as a natural part of life—or to teach them how to use failure advantageously. Fortunately, there are plenty of resources that can help you make wise choices. Seek learning opportunities outside the classroom and use this book as your ultimate teen guide. Above all, remember to be *human*. You don't have to delay the development of your individuality in order to achieve success. Be the person you want to be, TODAY. Be yourself, remain positive, and show respect for others. We are all in this together! You are now ready to take full control of your life. It's your *destiny* and your *rules*. Get out there and conquer the world!

References

"Are Teens Adopting Adults' Stress Habits?" American Psychological Association. Last modified February 11, 2014. https://www.apa.org/news/press/releases/stress/2013/teen-stress.

"Bullying Awareness & Prevention Guide." LearnPsychology. Last modified July 1, 2019. https://www.learnpsychology.org/now/bullying/.

"Exercise and Stress: Get Moving to Manage Stress." Mayo Clinic. Last modified March 8, 2018. https://www.mayoclinic.org/healthy-lifestyle/stress-management/in-depth/exercise-and-stress/art 20044469.

"Exposure Therapy." GoodTherapy. Last modified July 3, 2015. https://www.goodtherapy.org/learn-about-therapy/types/exposure-therapy.

"Get the Facts." National Organization for Women. Accessed August 11, 2019. https://now.org/now-foundation/love-your-body/love-your-body-whats-it-all-about/get-the-facts/.

Gordon, Sherri. "An Overview of Bullying." Verywell Family. Last modified February 5, 2018. https://www.verywellfamily.com/bullying-4157339.

Hoffses, Kathryn. "Test Anxiety." KidsHealth. Last modified July 2018. https://kidshealth.org/en/teens/test-anxiety.html.

"Isolation." GoodTherapy. Last modified August 20, 2018. https://www.goodtherapy.org/learn-about-therapy/issues/isolation.

Jewell, Tim. "Diaphragmatic Breathing and Its Benefits." Healthline. Last modified September 25, 2018. https://www.healthline.com/health/diaphragmatic-breathing.

Katz, Shirley. "Body Image." GoodTherapy. Last modified February 14, 2019. https://www.goodtherapy.org/learn-about-therapy/issues/body-image.

Lake, Monica. "The Importance of Social Skills: Raising a Socially Intelligent Child." GoodTherapy. Last modified January 2, 2018. https://www.goodtherapy.org/blog/importance-of-social-skills-raising-socially-intelligent-child-0102184.

Stewart, Emily. "Facebook Has Taken Down Billions of Fake Accounts, but the Problem is Still Getting Worse." Vox. Last modified May 23, 2019. https://www.vox.com/recode/2019/5/23/18637596/facebook-fake-accounts-transparency-mark-zuckerberg-report.

Terrell, Keith. "The History of Social Media: Social Networking Evolution!" History Cooperative. Last modified June 16, 2015. https://historycooperative.org/the-history-of-social-media/.

"Violence Awareness & Prevention Guide." LearnPsychology. Last modified July 1, 2019. https://www.learnpsychology.org/now/violence/.

Glossary of Terms

Adaptability	the quality of being able to adjust to new conditions
Assertiveness	the quality of being bold and confident through one's statements and behavior
Body dysmorphia	a psychological disorder in which a person becomes obsessed with imaginary defects in their appearance
Body image	the subjective picture or mental image of one's own body
Catfishing	the act of luring someone into a relationship by means of a fictional online persona
Cognitive behavioral therapy	a type of psychotherapy in which negative patterns of thought about the self and the world are challenged in order to alter unwanted behavior patterns or treat mood disorders such as depression
Collectivist culture	a culture that's based on valuing the needs of a group or of a community over the individual
Conflict resolution	the methods and processes that two or more parties use to find a peaceful solution to their dispute
Coping mechanism	the strategies people often use in the face of stress or trauma to help manage painful or difficult emotions
Cyberbullying	the use of electronic communication to bully a person, typically by sending messages of an intimidating or threatening nature
Diaphragmatic breathing	the practice of deep breathing accomplished by contracting the diaphragm—a muscle located horizontally between the thoracic cavity and abdominal cavity
Emotional intelligence	the capacity to be aware of, control, and express one's emotions, and to handle interpersonal relationships judiciously and empathetically

Empathy	the ability to understand and share the feelings of another
Endorphins	a hormone released by the brain that reduces pain and helps you feel relaxed and full of energy
Exposure therapy	a technique in behavior therapy that involves exposing the target patient to the anxiety source or its context without the intention to cause any danger
"Flight or fight" response	a psychological reaction that occurs in response to a perceived harmful event, attack, or threat to survival
Heartbreak	a feeling of overwhelming sadness and grief
Individualistic culture	a culture that prioritizes individuality and independence over a group mentality
Interpersonal skills	the qualities and behaviors a person uses to interact with others properly
Leadership	the art of motivating a group of people to act toward achieving a common goal
Peer pressure	a feeling that one must do the same things as other people of one's age and social group in order to be liked or respected by them
Performance anxiety	extreme nervousness experienced before or during participation in an activity taking place in front of an audience
Public speaking	the art of effective oral communication to a live audience
SMART goals	an acronym for goals that are "Specific, Measurable, Attainable, Relevant, and Timely"
Social cues	the subtle signals people send through their body language and expressions
Social skills	the learned abilities and behaviors needed to successfully work through the challenges of everyday life

Printed in Great Britain
by Amazon